Deadliest Mammals

Toney Allman

ReferencePoint Press®

San Diego, CA

© 2017 ReferencePoint Press, Inc.
Printed in the United States

For more information, contact:
ReferencePoint Press, Inc.
PO Box 27779
San Diego, CA 92198
www.ReferencePointPress.com

LIBRARY OF CONGRESS CATALOGING-IN-PUBLICATION DATA

Names: Allman, Toney, author.
Title: Deadliest mammals / Toney Allman.
Description: San Diego, CA : ReferencePoint Press, Inc., 2016. | Series:
  Deadliest predators | Includes bibliographical references and index.
Identifiers: LCCN 2016023812 (print) | LCCN 2016027148 (ebook) | ISBN
  9781682820506 (hardback) | ISBN 9781682820513 (eBook)
Subjects: LCSH: Carnivora--Juvenile literature.
Classification: LCC QL737.C2 A434 2016 (print) | LCC QL737.C2 (ebook) | DDC
  599.7--dc23
LC record available at https://lccn.loc.gov/2016023812

Contents

Born to Be Predators

Mammals are an incredibly diverse group of animals, with 5,416 species identified so far. The smallest mammal predator is Savi's white-toothed shrew, which lives in southern Europe, North Africa, and Asia. It measures just 2.4 inches (6 cm) long from its nose to the tip of its tail and weighs between .05 to .09 ounces (1.5 to 2.5 grams). By contrast, the carnivorous blue whale is not only the biggest mammal, reaching 100 feet (30 m) in length and 200 tons (181 metric tons), it is the biggest animal that has ever lived on Earth. The heaviest land mammal is the African elephant, weighing an average of 9.4 tons (8,500 kg), while the tallest animal is the male giraffe at 18 feet (5.5 m) tall. Of all the mammal species, about 270 are grouped in the order *Carnivora*, meaning they are predators, or flesh-eating mammals. In the order are twelve families. Nine of the families live on land and three are aquatic, called pinnipeds.

The Hunting Way of Life

Even in the order Carnivora, there is a lot of diversity, not just in where the animals live, but also in the characteristics that make them successful hunters. Many of them, for instance, also eat plants at times and thus are omnivorous, but almost all are meat eaters and depend on animal prey to survive. Carnivorous mammals live in almost every kind of habitat, from the tropics to the poles and in all the oceans. Most have teeth made for shearing and cutting, rather than grinding, and lower jaws that move up and down (for biting). They tend to have large brains relative to their size. Different predators may depend on any combination of keen senses (such as smell or eyesight), speed, claws, bite strength, stealth, and sheer power and size to capture the animals they hunt.

As a general rule, predators depend on hunting for survival. While many will also scavenge or steal prey from other predators, they also must hunt efficiently without risking injury to themselves from the struggles and bites, sharp hooves, or deadly horns of their prey. Commonly, this means singling out a prey animal that is young, injured, diseased, weak, or old because it is the safer animal to hunt, and the successful kill requires less expenditure of energy. Biologists call this "compensatory predation." Basically the predator is killing and eating the animals that would die anyway and helping to maintain the health of the prey species in the area. Even when a predator attacks an inattentive or lone healthy animal, the kill may help the prey species as well as the hungry predator. Those prey animals that are least capable of survival are culled from the group, and only the smartest and most alert live to pass their genes on to a new generation. In this way the habitat maintains enough food for the prey species to survive in healthy numbers.

Dangerous Hunger

The predator's preference for an easy kill, however, does not always keep healthy animals safe. Hunger is a powerful motivator, and predators are often very hungry.

Shrews, for example, hunt mostly insects, worms, and invertebrates, but every day, a shrew kills and eats the equivalent of its body weight. It is always on the hunt and must kill and eat every hour in order to survive. At the other end of the scale, the African lion does not need to hunt even daily. It will consume an average of 66 pounds (30 kg) of meat at one time and then not eat for several days. But the lion is such a powerful predator that when hunger drives it to hunt, no prey is safe from attack.

Predators are opportunistic about hunting, meaning that they will go for any easy kill that presents itself, but many have preferred prey. The lynx, for example, prefers snowshoe hares, and a cheetah's preference is for antelope and gazelles. No carnivore specifically hunts humans or prefers humans as prey. In fact, the mammals that are deadliest to human beings are not predators at all. More people die each year (about five thousand) in attacks from aggressive hippopotamuses defending territory than from carnivores on the hunt. But predatory attacks on humans do happen, mostly because people are in the wrong place at the wrong time. And even if the predator is attacking to protect itself, its territory, or its young rather than for food, the same characteristics that make it a successful hunter can make the encounter dangerous. When predator attacks on humans do happen, they are often fatal.

Predators Are Important

Preserves, national parks, and conservation areas have been established to protect both people and animals, but in many parts of the world, these areas are encroached upon by the spread of human communities, agricultural activity, poaching, and widespread tourism.

Most meat-eating mammals, including the polar bear, have teeth made for shearing and cutting rather than grinding. They also tend to have large brains relative to their size.

Loss of habitat, reductions in prey species, and human trespassing all lead to increased pressure on predators and make it harder for them to survive. No matter how fearsome some predators may be, their survival is important. Predators are a necessary and valuable part of the complex ecosystems in which they live. They help keep the environment in balance and stable, whether protecting it from the overgrazing of grasslands by herbivores, or ensuring the maximum fitness of prey populations by culling the weak and sick, or preventing the ecological system from being overrun by rodents. All the ecosystems of the earth need predators to remain healthy. When humans and dangerous predators have violent, deadly encounters, the immediate human response may be to wipe out the animals, but true predation on humans is rare. Most of the time, predator and human species are able to maintain an uneasy but peaceful coexistence.

Chapter 1

Lion

When lions in Africa treat humans like prey and seem to acquire a taste for human flesh, the lions are called "man-eaters." Perhaps the most famous man-eating lions were a pair of male lions that lived along the Tsavo River in Kenya during colonial times. The predation began when Indian construction crews, directed by Lieutenant Colonel John Henry Patterson, were hired by the British government to build a railroad bridge over the Tsavo River in March of 1898. Conditions were primitive and isolated, and almost immediately workers began to disappear. Patterson suspected lions when he found a mutilated body, but his efforts to stalk and shoot the lions failed. Every fence or trap that he erected failed to keep the lions out of the compound where the workers lived. By April, Patterson said, seventeen people had been dragged to their deaths. The two lions continued their predations until the workers were so terrorized that hundreds of them fled the site. Not until December of that year was Patterson able to shoot and kill the lions, and by that time, he claimed, the lions had killed and eaten 135 people. The man-eaters of Tsavo became legendary for their horrifying ferocity.

The lions killed by Patterson were stuffed and sold to the Field Museum in Chicago, Illinois, where modern-day scientists have tested their hair samples for proof of man-eating. While Patterson may have exaggerated the numbers, the museum researchers were able to estimate that one lion had eaten ten people and the other, twenty-four. In addition, they discovered that one of the lions suffered with severe dental disease and a jaw injury. The lion may have turned to humans for food because it was too weak to hunt its usual prey—and people were easy marks. But 1898 did not see the end of lion attacks on humans in the Tsavo region. The descendants of the Tsavo lions continue to threaten the people of the area today. In 2015, during the rebuilding of the same railway line, a guard was badly mauled by a Tsavo lion. The man was saved when other guards shot and killed the lion. Estimates of lion attacks in Tsavo vary, but every year there are at least one or two reports of local people killed by lions in the region.

Body Basics

Lions, which are Africa's top predators, are built for killing large prey. Male lions can weigh up to 496 pounds (225 kg) with an average height at the shoulder of 4 feet (1.2 m). Their body length, not including the tail can be 10.8 feet (3.3 m). Females are slightly smaller, weighing up to 330 pounds (150 kg) and standing an average of 3.6 feet (1.1 m) tall. With powerful muscles, lions can leap up to 36 feet (11 m) and run short sprints at 37 miles per hour (60 kph). Depending on their habitats, lions have coats colored tawny gold or darker so that they easily blend in with brush or tall grass on the savannas, plains, and scrublands where they live. Despite their size, they are so well camouflaged that they can be incredibly difficult to see.

The lion's most formidable weapons are its teeth and claws. Lions have three kinds of specialized teeth: incisors in the front for tearing and gripping meat; four canines for tearing and slashing that can be 2.8 inches (7 cm) long; and carnassial teeth at the back of the mouth that are as sharp as scissors for cutting flesh. Extremely strong retractable claws can grow up to 1.5 inches (3.8 cm) long, and lions keep the claws sharp by scratching them on trees. Even a lion's tongue is powerful; it is so rough that it can lick off skin or remove meat from bones with a few strokes. Lions also have acute senses. Their night vision is eight times better than a human's, and

The lion is the top predator on the African continent. Powerful muscles and the ability to run short, swift sprints help to make the lion a formidable foe.

THE LION
AT A GLANCE

- **Scientific name:** *Panthera leo*
- **Scientific family:** Felidae
- **Range:** Sub-Saharan Africa
- **Habitat:** Savannas, open plains, semideserts, and thick bush
- **Average size:** 3.5 to 4 feet (1 to 1.2 m) at the shoulder
- **Diet:** Large herd animals
- **Life span:** Ten to fourteen years in the wild
- **Key features:** The only social cats; live in prides and hunt collaboratively
- **Deadly because:** Large size, strength, and powerful teeth and claws
- **Conservation status:** Vulnerable (population decreasing)

their ears can pick up the sound of prey a mile away. In the roof of a lion's mouth is an organ called the Jacobson's organ, which allows the animal to taste the air and pick up the smell of prey. It is little wonder that when a lion roars, every living thing within hearing distance stops and listens.

Home and Living Habits

A thousand years ago, lions roamed throughout Africa, Asia, southern Europe, and the Middle East. Today, with only about twenty thousand to thirty thousand left in the wild, they are mostly confined to parts of southern Africa, usually in game parks and preserves. Lions are the only social cats. Groups of related females and young along with one to three males live in groups known as prides, which average about fifteen members. Males establish and maintain the pride's territory, while females do most of the hunting, either cooperatively or alone. Territories are hunting ranges and may be as large as 100 square miles (259 sq km). For the most part, lions sleep during the day and are active at night.

On the Hunt

Large herd animals such as zebra, wildebeest, and antelope are the lion's preferred prey, although when hungry they will hunt any animals available, scavenge, or steal kills from other predators. Lions are stealth hunters and stalk their prey. When hunting as a group, they encircle the prey, each lion creeping as close as possible. Then one or more lions charge when within about 100 feet (30 m) of the selected animal. If the first rush fails, the prey usually gets away since lions do not have the stamina to sustain a chase for long. In a successful hunt, the lion leaps upon the back of the animal, using its weight to drag the prey down while biting at its spine. Once the animal is down, lions bite the throat or nose and mouth to suffocate it as quickly as possible. All the lions of the pride gorge on the kill, but only in turn. The adult males eat first, then the adult females, and finally (if anything is left) the cubs and young. Lions will fight over a kill and access to the flesh, so it is every lion for itself as each member of the group strives to get a portion of the food. Unless the prey animal is large, often the weak and the young get nothing.

Lions generally hunt and eat only every three or four days, but when conditions are good and prey animals are plentiful, a single lion can eat up to 110 pounds (50 kg) of meat at one time. Over the course of a year, a lion's intake averages to about 11 to 15 pounds (5 to 7 kg) of meat a day. Lions may also go on killing sprees when the opportunity arises. In 1964, for example, during a severe drought that badly weakened many herd animals, a pride of lions was observed killing fifteen buffalo in the Punda Maria area of South Africa. It was much more than the pride could eat, but the lions did not stop until all the animals were dead. This behavior is one factor that makes lions so deadly. The pride will not leave any animal (or human) that has been attacked until it is dead.

A Zimbabwe national park employee examines the teeth of an African lion. Lions have three sets of teeth—one set for tearing and gripping, one set for tearing and slashing, and one set for cutting.

MALE HUNTING STRATEGIES

Female lions stalk prey cooperatively, and males usually appear only after the prey is killed in order to take the first and largest shares. However, male lions are not completely dependent on female hunting. Male lions can be skillful hunters, too. Instead of hunting together, the males hunt alone. And instead of stalking, they use ambush techniques. By night, a male lion will lie hidden in dense brush or other vegetation and wait for a prey animal to come along. Then it leaps on the animal from behind. For the big male lions the tactic is quite successful. Vulnerable prey never see the menace that is hiding in the tall grass or brush, and the lion can gorge without sharing his feast.

Attacks on Humans

Lions seem to view humans as other predators and usually avoid contact with people when possible. However, lions will attack humans when threatened or hungry. They sometimes come to see people as prey, either because they develop a taste for human flesh or because they learn that humans are easy targets. Throughout Africa, about one hundred people are killed by lions each year, but that number is relatively low because most lions in Africa are now living in game parks and preserves. In southern Tanzania and northern Mozambique—some of the last areas left where humans and lions live side by side—about 140 lion attacks are reported every year. Poor villagers in these places at times live in terrible fear of man-eating lions grabbing unwary children at play or

A female lion grabs a zebra by the throat, a technique that leads to a quick death. All of the lions in the pride will gorge on the kill.

tearing through a thatched roof to steal a sleeping victim. Craig Packer, a professor at the University of Minnesota and a lion expert, explains,

> There are parts of Africa where humans are just another meal. . . . Regardless of their initial experience with human flesh, once lions learn that people can be eaten, some become repeat offenders. Some habitual man-eaters are males, some are females, some are old, and some are young. Sometimes whole prides partake.[1]

Some villagers in parts of Africa practice revenge killings on lions when the lions attack humans or the village livestock. Throughout most of Africa it is illegal to kill a lion without government permission, but villagers will do so when their lives or livelihoods are threatened. In general humans are a greater threat to lions than lions are to people today. Nevertheless in its element the lion is still the top predator, and humans who forget to take precautions can fall victim whether the lion is hungry or not.

In 2015, for instance, tour guide Quinn Swales was killed by a male lion while leading a group of tourists on a walking safari in Hwange National Park in Zimbabwe. The lion boldly walked toward Swales, charged and leapt on him, and bit him on the shoulder and neck. Swales had placed himself between the tourists and the lion. He had set off a "bear banger"—a loud firecracker-like flare—to scare off the lion, but nothing he did stalled the lion's attack. Swales died at the scene. Luke Dollar of National Geographic's Big Cats Initiative says of the incident,

> Almost any organism around lions might be a potential prey item, and for people to think that they are an exception is folly. . . . We need to remember that we call these animals the kings of the jungles for a reason. We need to respect what they are and their natural behaviors.[2]

Even in parks, humans cannot have a false sense of security about the animal that is one of the deadliest predators in the world.

Chapter 2

Tiger

The world's deadliest mammals rarely prefer human flesh to other animals, but it does happen. The single mammal predator that killed and ate the most humans ever in history was a Bengal tiger. She was known as the Champawat tigress. During the late nineteenth century, she roamed in Nepal, where she apparently had been shot and wounded and therefore was unable to hunt her usual prey. The tigress began preying on humans almost exclusively and reportedly killed and ate two hundred people before the Nepalese government sent the army to kill the dangerous beast. The army failed, but with all the activity she was driven from her territory and crossed into the Champawat region of India. There she was credited with killing and eating another 236 people before she was stopped. She was shot and killed in 1911 by the famous tiger hunter Jim Corbett. In a book he wrote about his adventures, Corbett explains one reason that tigers such as the Champawat tigress are so dangerous. He says, "When a tiger becomes a man-eater it loses all fear of human beings and, as human beings move about more freely in the day than they do at night, it is able to secure its victims during daylight hours."[3]

In Corbett's day, more than one hundred thousand tigers of nine different subspecies (such as the Bengal and Sumatran) roamed in Asia. Today, with three subspecies extinct, only about thirty-two hundred are left in the wild.

Their small numbers, however, do not mean that tigers are not still deadly to humans at times. In India, where half the remaining tigers live, about eighty-five tiger attacks on humans are reported each year. In 2014, for example, seventeen people were killed by tigers in five weeks in four different northern Indian states. Humans continue to fall victim to those rare tigers that become true man-eaters.

Body Basics

Tigers are the largest members of the cat family. Five sub-species of tigers are left in the wild: Bengal, Indochinese, Siberian, Sumatran, and Malayan. (The South China tiger survives, but only in zoos.) Of these, the largest is the Siberian, with males weighing between 400 and 675

The Siberian tiger (pictured) is the world's largest cat. All tigers have powerful muscles that enable them to spring on prey animals and knock them to the ground.

pounds (181 to 306 kg), while Sumatrans are the smallest, weighing about 220 to 310 pounds (100 to 136 kg). Bengals, the most numerous subspecies, average 490 pounds (222 kg). Females of all subspecies are smaller. Tigers average about 3 feet (1 m) tall at the shoulder and may measure from 4.6 to 9.2 feet (1.4 to 2.8 m) long, not including the tail. Tigers have thick orange coats with white markings and white bellies and stripes of black or brown for camouflage.

A tiger's build is extremely muscular and powerful. With longer hind legs than front legs, it is an excellent jumper, able to reach up to 32.5 feet (10 m) in one leap. Tigers can climb trees and are also excellent swimmers. Tiger claws are retractable, curved, and sharp, and can reach up to 4 inches (10 cm) in length. The tiger's thirty teeth also are formidable hunting weapons. The canine teeth, or fangs, can grow to 3 inches (7.6 cm) long and are equipped with many nerves that sense pressure and help the tiger locate the right place to deliver a killing bite. The back teeth are called carnassials. They are like knife blades that allow the tiger to shear large chunks of meat from its prey and then swallow the chunks without further chewing. A large gap between the carnassials and the canine teeth enables the tiger to bite deeply into its prey and tightly grip struggling animals. Even the small teeth in the front of the mouth are useful hunting tools. They allow the tiger to pick small pieces of meat off the bone or pluck feathers from prey.

Home and Habits

Today, tiger populations are generally confined to northeastern China, Southeast Asia, far eastern Russia, and several parts of India. They live in a variety of different

THE TIGER
AT A GLANCE

- **Scientific name:** *Panthera tigris*
- **Scientific family:** Felidae
- **Range:** South and Southeast Asia, far eastern Russia, and China
- **Habitat:** Widely varied, from tropical forests to savannas and tundra, to swamps or mountains
- **Average size:** 4.6 to 9.2 feet (1.4 to 2.8 m) long
- **Diet:** Deer, pigs, buffalo, and antelope
- **Life span:** Average ten to fifteen years in the wild
- **Key features:** Strength and power; largest of the cat family
- **Deadly because:** Great size, powerful muscles, and strong, sharp teeth and claws
- **Conservation status:** Endangered

habitats, including rain forests, mountains, grasslands, swamps, and even icy tundra. Tigers usually live solitary lives and hunt alone. They are most active at night, which is when they hunt. Each tiger maintains and defends a territory that is regularly scent-marked with urine, but male territories can overlap with several female territories. The size of the territory depends on the prey animals available. Fewer animals to hunt requires larger territories. Bengal tigers typically find all the prey they need in an area of about 20 square miles (51.8 sq km). Siberian tigers, in contrast, may claim a territory as large as 463 square miles (1,200 sq km) because so few prey animals live in the vast woodlands that are their home. Both male and female tigers maintain several dens within their territories. Tigers are social only during mating season and when females are raising young. Young tigers stay with their mothers until they are at least two-and-a-half years old.

A tiger's claws (pictured) are curved and extremely sharp. The claws, feet, and leg bones shown here come from a tiger killed by a poacher.

On the Hunt

Only about one of every twenty hunts is successful, so tigers often go several days at a time without eating. When a hunt is successful, a tiger can eat 80 pounds (36 kg) of meat at one time. Tigers depend on eyesight and hearing rather than smell to find and attack prey. They are solitary hunters and typically use stalk-and-ambush strategies. First they circle upwind of a targeted victim so that the prey will not be warned off by their scent. Then slowly and patiently they sneak as close to the rear of a prey animal as possible. Finally they leap forward, knocking the animal to the ground, grabbing the victim's back or shoulders with front claws and sharp teeth and deliver a killing bite to the neck or throat. If the prey animal is very large, the tiger may clamp its jaws around the neck in a stranglehold and suffocate the animal. Suffocation usually takes about ninety seconds, and the tiger will hold the bite until no movement remains. Alternatively, a tiger may ambush hunt, lying in wait by a waterhole, for example, and then springing upon any animal that passes by.

Preferred tiger prey includes deer, wild pigs, water buffalo, and antelope, but they will also eat smaller animals such as hares, porcupines, reptiles, and monkeys. They have also been known to attack and eat elephant calves, leopards, and sloth bears. After a kill, the tiger typically carries or drags the meal into dense brush or cover before it begins feeding. If the tiger is unable to finish a large meal, it covers the remains with dirt and grass to hide the kill from scavengers. It will return to the meal to finish it over the next few days. It is estimated that a tiger will consume the equivalent of about fifty full-grown deer every year.

When Tigers Attack Humans

Most tigers are wary of humans. Jim Corbett writes, "A man-eating tiger is a tiger that has been compelled, through stress of circumstances beyond its control, to adopt a diet alien to it. The stress of circumstances is, in nine cases out of ten, wounds, and in the tenth case old age."[4] For the most part, this assessment is still true, although some healthy tigers will attack humans because people have encroached on the tiger's territory, in preserves or in wild tiger habitats. At other times, tigers have developed a taste for human flesh because of scavenging dead bodies, perhaps after a hurricane or other natural disaster.

Geoffrey Ward, a *National Geographic* writer who spent his boyhood in India, says that many attacks on

A Bengal tiger feeds on a deer. Tigers hunt by stalking or ambushing their prey.

DEATH AT THE ZOO

Stacey Konwiser, the lead tiger keeper at the Palm Beach Zoo in Florida, was killed by one of her charges on April 15, 2016. Konwiser was an experienced handler of tigers, and the tiger that attacked her had been reared all his life in zoos. Nevertheless, when Konwiser made the mistake of entering the tiger's night enclosure when its door had not been secured, the tiger entered and attacked. Konwiser was alone at the time, so no one saw what happened. Other zoo personnel described the tiger as highly territorial and not friendly. It made no difference that it had been raised around people. The coroner who did the autopsy confirmed that Konwiser had died of neck injuries (in keeping with how tigers kill their prey). Captive big cats always pose a threat to their keepers and are never truly tamed or domesticated.

humans are accidents, caused by the tiger mistaking a human for natural prey. He explains,

> Human beings walking upright and sticking to forest roads are relatively safe, then; it is when they wander off into the undergrowth and lean over, cutting grass or collecting firewood, so that they lose their distinctively human look, that the likelihood of tragic error seems to intensify.[5]

The trouble is that such an accident can teach a tiger that humans are easy prey.

In the Sundarbans, a mangrove swamp stretching across the borders of eastern West Bengal, India, and southern Bangladesh, tigers kill more people than any other place on Earth. Ward says that about one of every three of the two hundred to five hundred Bengal tigers in the Sundarbans is an opportunistic man-eater, meaning that it will attack and eat any human it happens upon. The people who live in the Sundarbans are fishermen, farmers, honey hunters, and woodcutters, and on average about fifty of them are killed by tigers every year. No one knows why the tigers of the Sundarbans are so aggressive and willing to attack people, but the stories of predation are horrifying. In 2014, for instance, sixty-two-year-old Sushil Majhi was crabbing from his boat in a jungle-lined creek with his son and daughter. A tiger suddenly leaped from the bank into the boat and grabbed Majhi by the neck. The son and daughter beat at the tiger with a stick and a cutting tool, but it was no use. Majhi's son later said, "It [the tiger] jumped off and landed on the bank in one giant leap. We saw it disappear into the jungle with my father still in its jaws."[6] The victim's body was never found.

When tigers attack humans, they use the same method as with other prey. They stalk their victims from behind, leap onto the shoulders of the bent over or sitting human, knock the prey down with their weight, and then deliver a killing bite to the head or neck. Knowing that tigers do not like to approach prey face-to-face, people in the Sundarbans began wearing brightly painted masks of faces with big eyes on the backs of their heads when they entered the jungles. The masks were designed to fool the tigers, but the trick worked for only about two or three years. And still, every village in the Sundarbans has at least one tiger widow—a woman who has lost a husband to a tiger attack. Other animals (such as snakes) in India and Bangladesh kill many more people than tigers do, but it is tigers that cause fear and horror when one goes after humans.

Chapter 3

Polar Bear

Because of its immense size, strength, and power, the polar bear is one of the most dangerous predators alive. It is almost purely carnivorous and is ideally equipped for hunting, not only with large teeth and claws but also with a sense of smell that can detect prey from 0.6 of a mile (1 km) away and under 3.3 feet (1 m) of frozen snow. A polar bear hunting a seal can take the whole head in its jaws and then whip the body of the 150-pound (70 kg) animal out of the water and onto the ice. Polar bears are also intelligent and adaptable. They have been observed running through a herd of walruses resting on shore to panic the animals. As the 2,000-pound (907 kg) walruses rush into the sea, they inadvertently trample some of their pups. Then, the polar bear eats the pups.

Every animal in the Arctic fears the polar bear. It is widely acknowledged to be the largest carnivore on land, and in its environment, it is at the top of the food chain, with no other animals preying upon it. A polar bear fearlessly attacks any creature in the face of a threat or for food.

Body Basics

Polar bears have evolved to be perfectly suited to their Arctic environment. They are the largest bears on Earth, with males weighing on average between 775 and 1,300 pounds (350 to 600 kg) and height at the shoulder at 3.5 to 5 feet (1 to 1.5 m). When standing on its hind legs, a polar bear may be more than 10 feet (3 m) tall. Females are smaller but can reach more than 700 pounds (318 kg) and 6 to 7 feet (1.8 to 2.1 m) in length. The bears

Because of its immense size, strength, and power, the polar bear is one of the most dangerous predators on Earth. A polar bear driven by hunger or threat will fearlessly attack any creature in its path.

THE POLAR BEAR
AT A GLANCE

- Scientific name: *Ursus maritimus*
- Scientific family: Ursidae
- Range: Circumpolar Arctic
- Habitat: Sea ice, ocean waters, islands, and coastlines
- Average size: Head and body length 7.25 to 8 feet (2.2 to 2.4 m)
- Diet: Ice seals
- Life span: Fifteen to twenty years
- Key features: Biggest land carnivore, with fur and fat layers ideally suited to Arctic existence
- Deadly because: Huge, strong, intelligent animal with powerful teeth and claws
- Conservation status: Vulnerable

have excellent senses of sight, hearing, and smell and forty-two long, sharp teeth for tearing into and chewing flesh. All healthy polar bears have two layers of dense fur and a thick layer of fat to protect them from the cold. Even their feet have fur between the toes and pads.

Although polar bears have somewhat short legs for their size, their paws are very large and strong. The front paws are rounded, while the rear paws are somewhat elongated. A polar bear's front paws are so powerful that one swipe can kill an animal or a person. The paws measure about 1 foot (31 cm) across and help the bear to distribute its weight when walking on thin ice, to swim in the ocean by acting like paddles, and to catch prey. The bottoms of their feet have small bumps called *papillae* that prevent them from slipping on ice. Thick, strong, curved claws, up to 2 inches (5.1 cm) in length, provide additional traction on the ice and grab and hold on to prey.

Polar bears are excellent swimmers. With long bodies, pointed noses, and long necks, they swim easily and swiftly. They can swim for hours at a time, using the front paws to move forward and the longer back paws as rudders for steering. One female polar bear was discovered to have swum for nine days without stopping, covering 426 miles (687 km). Polar bears are fast swimmers as well. They have been clocked at 6 miles per hour (9.7 kph) in the water. In contrast, the average human can swim about 3 miles per hour (4.8 kph).

Home and Habits

Polar bears live on Arctic land masses and seas where annual ice packs cover the ocean, but they spend the majority of their lives on the sea ice. They are the only bears to be classified as marine mammals. They are found in Alaska, Canada, Russia, Greenland, and Norway. During the summer months, when the polar ice recedes, the bears are forced to stay on land, often fasting and surviving on their fat reserves since enough food is difficult to find. Unlike other bears, polar bears do not hibernate; they remain active all year long. However, they prefer to move slowly, nap frequently, and use as little energy as possible, both to avoid overheating and to conserve energy reserves.

During the winter months, polar bears roam the ice, often swimming from ice floe to ice floe in search of food. Except for mothers with cubs, they tend to live solitary lives. They may get together with other bears for mating or when a number of bears discover a large food source, such as a dead, beached whale. At those times, bears may communicate with each other through growls, grumbles, and body language that asks the bear that found the food to be willing to share.

As global temperatures warm and summer conditions last longer, sea ice is retreating. Polar bears end up spending more time on land and less on the sea ice that is their

A polar bear's paw (pictured) is so large and powerful that it can kill an animal or human with a single swipe. Its strong, sharp claws help it walk on ice and grab and hold prey.

DETERMINATION

Wildlife cameraman Gordon Buchanan was shooting a BBC documentary about polar bears in Norway in 2012. He had set up his equipment on the ice inside a clear, five-sided, metal-framed protective pod called a Perspex box, so that he could film an Arctic polar bear family in safety. That was when the 1,000-pound (454 kg) polar bear came for him. She was starving and had two cubs to feed as well. For forty-five minutes, the bear tried to break into the box to seize her prey. He had a close-up view of the huge bear's jaws, teeth, and claws as she determinedly sought a way to get at him. He heard her roar in frustration. Buchanan kept filming and talking throughout the assault. He remembers,

> Without a doubt she wanted me for lunch. She was so persistent, looking for a weak spot for almost 45 minutes. I was terrified and you could hear my heartbeat on the mic [microphone]. It really was a sensational moment and a worrying situation. It shows how enormous and powerful they are. . . . It is the most difficult thing I have done and the scariest.

Quoted in Harriet Arkell, "So THAT'S What It's Like to Be Eaten by a Polar Bear! Photographer Inches from Animal's Jaws as He Takes Wildlife Shots from Safety of Perspex Cage," *Daily Mail*, January 4, 2013. www.dailymail.co.uk.

natural habitat. Some scientists blame these changes for the occasional cannibalism that has been observed in polar bears. They have been seen attacking and eating other bears and bear cubs during summer months when they are trapped on land and often starving. In 2010, for instance, photojournalist Jenny Ross witnessed a male polar bear eating a juvenile one. She comments,

This type of intraspecific predation has always occurred to some extent. However, there are increasing numbers of observations of it occurring, particularly on land where polar bears are trapped ashore, completely food-deprived for extended periods of time due to the loss of sea ice as a result of climate change.[7]

On the Hunt

A polar bear's natural prey is seals, particularly ringed seals and bearded seals. These so-called ice seals also depend on sea ice to survive. The seals spend most of their time in the ocean, but they make breathing holes in the ice to be used when needed, rest on ice floes, and raise their young in dens of snow on ice that juts out from shores. A polar bear's main hunting strategy with seals is still-hunting. The polar bear uses its sense of smell to locate a breathing hole actively used by a seal. Then the bear waits patiently by the hole, sometimes for hours or even days, for the seal to stick its head up to take a breath. The bear grabs the seal by its head and pulls it from the water. A polar bear also will stalk seals resting on the ice. The bear will slowly creep forward toward the seal, freezing in place every time the seal lifts its head. Once close enough, the bear rushes forward and pounces on the seal before it can slip back into the water. Polar bears also hunt seal pups, locating the ice and snow dens by smell, crashing through the roofs of the dens, and then eating the pups inside.

When hunting is good, polar bears eat only the seal blubber, or fat, and leave the remains for scavengers, such as foxes, ravens, and younger bears. Seal fat is the richest source of calories and energy available in the polar bear's environment—one bear can eat 100 pounds (45 kg) of blubber at a time. Seal blubber is necessary for the polar bear to sustain and build up its own fat reserves. During the summer months, when seals are scarce, polar bears will eat anything they can find, including birds, small mammals, eggs, berries from tundra shrubs, and even human garbage. These other food sources do not provide enough calories to sustain polar bears because they do not have enough fat. Polar bears live a feast-or-famine existence, but as long as the sea ice returns every fall, they are able to survive and thrive.

Deadly Encounters with Humans

During the summer polar bears spend time on land and may encounter humans, either in isolated human settlements, such as Barrow, Alaska, or when people take treks and tours to see Arctic wildlife. Polar bears have been so geographically isolated that they have not developed a fear of humans. When they do encounter humans, the bears see the same thing they see in any animal: a possible meal. Although fatal attacks on humans are rare (only about three occur each year), encounters between polar bears and people can be extremely dangerous. Usually the only way anyone survives a polar bear attack is if someone shoots and kills the bear. Matt Dyer's story is the exception. Both he and the polar bear survived an attack in the summer of 2013. Dyer was one of a group of seven people on a Sierra Club hiking and camping trip about 560 miles (901 km) south of the Arctic Circle in the Torngat Mountains National Park in Labrador, Canada. The experienced group knew that polar bears were a danger. They set up their tents

A polar bear drags away its kill—a seal. Polar bears will sometimes wait for hours or days at a hole in the ice; when a seal finally surfaces for air, the polar bear will pounce.

inside an electrified wire fence that they strung around the camp before they went to sleep. At 2:30 a.m., Dyer awoke to realize that the fence had been no deterrent at all. The giant silhouette of a polar bear loomed over his tent. Suddenly it ripped a hole in the nylon cloth and clamped its jaws around Dyer's head from left temple to right jaw, crushing his vocal cords and puncturing his scalp. The bear threw Dyer around and yanked his whole body through the hole. Then, gripping Dyer tightly, the bear raced off toward a nearby river. Dyer remained conscious, but he was sure he could not be saved. He remembers thinking to himself, "We all die. This is it. You're going home."[8]

Everyone else in the camping party was awake and screaming at the sight of Dyer's limp body dangling from the receding polar bear's mouth. The group's leader shot his flare gun at the bear. Two shots finally forced the bear to drop Dyer and escape the scene. He was badly injured and would have died but for the fact that one of the other campers was a physician. He treated Dyer's many bite wounds before a rescue helicopter arrived to take Dyer to the hospital. After much surgery and rehabilitation treatment, Dyer healed, although his voice is permanently changed because of the damage to his vocal cords, and his left hand does not work completely normally. He is glad the bear was unharmed, but he knows he is extremely fortunate to be alive. The polar bear snatched Dyer just as it would have grabbed a seal. Once in a polar bear's powerful grasp, few living things escape being eaten.

Chapter 4

Wolverine

At only the size of a medium dog, the wolverine is not a threat to humans, and there are no well-documented cases of any attacks on humans. The wolverine earns its status as a deadly mammal because of its fierce, fearless, tireless, voracious aggression and because of its strength in comparison to its size. This largest member of the weasel family can defend itself, its territory, and its kill against much larger animals. It has a reputation of never backing down from a confrontation, and as a predator, it is both efficient and deadly.

Body Basics

Despite its relationship to weasels, the wolverine looks like a small bear. It has a broad head, with small eyes and short, rounded ears. Its long, dark-brown, water-repellent hair covers a body that measures 26 to 34 inches (66 to 86 cm) long from its head to the root of its tail. The bushy, furred tail is 7 to 10 inches (18 to 25 cm) long. The legs are short, and the body has a long yellowish or whitish stripe down both sides. The paws are broad and act like snowshoes. They have tough, hooked claws for digging, climbing trees, defense, and grabbing and tearing at prey. The face has a distinctive lighter brown mask on the forehead and eyes. Native

Americans of the Blackfeet tribe named the wolverine the "skunk bear." The skunk part of the name is in reference to the smelly yellow liquid a wolverine can release from its anal glands. The scent is used to mark territory, warn other wolverines away, and in defense if the wolverine feels threatened.

Wolverines weigh no more than about 35 pounds (15.9 kg), with males larger than females, but they are powerful animals. The teeth and jaws of a wolverine are incredibly strong for their size. The upper molars in the back of the wolverine's mouth are rotated inward at 90 degrees. This special characteristic, along with the bite strength of the jaws, enables a wolverine to bite through frozen meat and crush bone. Wolverines also have endurance. Scientist Howard Golden describes wolverines as fast, agile travelers with the stamina to cover long distances under severe conditions. He says, "They go up and down really steep, icy, rocky slopes like they're not even there. You could never hike it—you'd need climbing gear."[9]

Home and Behavior

Wolverines need the ability to scale the roughest, iciest terrains because they live in northern circumpolar regions, such as Alaska, Canada, Norway, Sweden, Finland, and Russia. They are also found in the North Cascades and Rocky Mountains in the mainland United States. They live in alpine and boreal forests, tundra, and grasslands, as well as at or above the timberline in remote mountainous areas. Wolverines are at home in deep snow, on icy crags, and in frozen tundra. In these harsh conditions they need large territories in which to roam because the environment supports only sparse populations of prey animals. One wolverine was record-

A wolverine walks through a snow-covered landscape in Russia. Wolverines are aggressive, fierce, and fearless—all of which makes them formidable predators.

ed traveling a total of 550 miles (885 km) in forty-two days. Wolverines are not numerous in any environment, even when their populations are healthy, and they live mostly solitary lives. Males, however, maintain territories that overlap several female territories. The females build dens of snow to rear their young, and the males will often visit these dens to interact with the offspring and help raise them. Much is unknown about wolverine behavior because they are so reclusive and so sparsely distributed in their habitats.

THE WOLVERINE
AT A GLANCE

- **Scientific name:** *Gulo gulo*
- **Scientific family:** Mustelidae
- **Range:** Canada, Estonia, Finland, Mongolia, Norway, Russia, Sweden, and the United States
- **Habitat:** Remote northern latitudes in Arctic, subarctic, alpine, and boreal forests
- **Average size:** About 35 pounds (15.8 kg)
- **Diet:** Rodents, sheep, goat, deer, caribou, moose
- **Life span:** Five to thirteen years
- **Key features:** Looks like a small bear, skunk-like secretions, high stamina
- **Deadly because:** Fearless, fierce, determined, and with a voracious appetite
- **Conservation status:** Least concern, vulnerable, and endangered, depending on the region

Wolverines do not hibernate. Throughout the year they are active during the day, but most prefer to hunt at night. Although wolverines eat eggs, berries, and vegetation, they prefer meat and seek out prey whenever they can. Wolverines are often called *gluttons* (their scientific name *gulo* is Latin for "glutton") — and for good reason. Wolverines have huge appetites. They kill prey even when they are full and store the extra meat in caches of deep snow. Even when caches are full and the wolverine is gorged, it will kill if the opportunity presents itself. A wolverine never stops hunting for meat.

On the Hunt

Wolverines are both scavengers and hunters, and they will also steal kills from other predators. Being opportunistic eaters, they will eat any animal flesh they can find. Their diet includes squirrels, rabbits, hares, porcupines, marmots, mice, shrews, beaver, sheep, goats, deer, caribou, moose, and even other predators such as lynx and small bears. A wolverine can smell small mammals in their burrows 20 feet (6 m) under the snow, quickly dig down with its sharp claws, and snatch the hibernating animals. If an animal carcass is frozen under an avalanche, the wolverine can smell it and dig it up easily. When a large animal is foundering in deep snow, the

A growling wolverine pokes its head out of a den. Wolverines can crush bone and bite through frozen meat thanks to their incredibly strong teeth and jaws and the angle of their molars.

wolverine—with its snowshoe-like feet—can race atop the snow, leap on its back, bite and slash its neck until it chokes and falls down, and then disembowel it. An injured animal of any size is also an opportunity for a meal; the wolverine will attack and slash viciously, refusing to let go or give up until the prey is dead. Then it will eat the entire animal, including bones, hooves, and even teeth.

Wolverines are fearless when trying to get a meal, and that means that they will stand up to and fight much larger predators in order to steal a fresh kill or to protect their own kills from other animals—even bears, cougars, and wolves. Larger predators, such as wolves and mountain lions, often go for several days without a meal, but the wolverine must eat every day. Perhaps that need accounts for its determination, tenacity, and ferocity when confronting another predator over a kill. Wolverines have been observed threatening and attacking grizzly bears and packs of wolves in order to attain meat. And they often win. Naturalist George Bird Grinnell recorded a wolverine story told to him by an Alaskan hunter in 1926 of a wolverine fighting a grizzly bear that was trying to steal the wolverine's freshly killed caribou. According to the hunter, the wolverine mortally wounded the bear in the fight. The bear moved off and died about 300 yards (274 m) from the caribou carcass. The hunter discovered that the bear had been disemboweled, but he did not know if the wolverine had done this before or after the bear was dead.

Wolverines do not always win their fights. In 2002, in Yellowstone National Park, researchers Kristine and Bob Inman found a wolverine that they had been tracking lying dead beside an elk carcass. The wolverine had been killed by a black bear when it tried to steal the

SUMMING UP THE WOLVERINE

In his 2010 book *The Wolverine Way*, biologist Douglas Chadwick describes wolverines as animals that live "fiercely and relentlessly." He explains,

> If wolverines have a strategy, it's this: Go hard, and high, and steep, and never back down, not even from the biggest grizzly, and least of all from a mountain. Climb everything: trees, cliffs, avalanche chutes, summits. Eat everything: alive, dead, long-dead, moose, mouse, fox, frog, its still-warm heart or frozen bones.

Chadwick spent years tracking and studying wolverines, and he came to admire them for their fascinating abilities to survive and their tough, strong spirits. He says they are symbols of the wilderness.

Douglas Chadwick, *The Wolverine Way*, Ventura, CA: Patagonia Books, 2010, p. 47.

bear's kill. Kristine Inman says, "This incident, where a wolverine decided to battle it out head-on with another carnivore ten times his size, substantiates the species' ferocious and intrepid reputation."[10] Most often, according to animal researchers, other predators back off from a fight with a snarling, growling, threatening wolverine. The wolverine is so fiercely determined and fearless that fighting over a kill is not worth the risk.

Wolverine Lore

Throughout history, wolverines have developed the reputation of being the toughest, fiercest mammals in the wilderness. Because they are so reclusive and hard to study, many tales of their viciousness have been told that are difficult for scientists to verify. However, the stories are impressive. In 2014, for example, Craig Johnson survived for three days in the Alaskan wilderness when his

A wolverine feasts on an animal carcass in the midst of a Russian winter. Whether they hunt their own prey or scavenge prey killed by another animal, wolverines are both savage and dangerous.

snowmobile crashed through ice into the water. Johnson was injured and freezing and had to walk for 30 miles (48.3 km) to get help. He said a wolverine stalked him the whole way. Despite firing his gun toward the animal, he could not scare it away. Johnson remembers, "You could hear it on the ice, just playing with me, toying with me."[11] He armed himself with a stick in case he had to fight off the wolverine's attack in close quarters when he tried to shelter in a box he had found. Whether it would really have leaped on him is unknown, but Johnson was sure he was in mortal danger.

Many people have claimed that wolverines will attack humans, but there has never been scientific confirmation of a wolverine attacking a human; however, tales of successful attacks on animals larger than humans are common in history. During the 1930s one researcher reported on a wolverine at a zoo that was placed in an enclosure with a polar bear. He claimed that the wolverine immediately killed the bear. Another story from the early twentieth century is about the intelligence and cruelty of the wolverine. The tale is related by environmentalist and sportsman Mark Allardyce. The story goes that a wolverine will hunt by climbing a tree with a quantity of moss in its mouth and wait for a deer to pass under the tree. When the deer comes close, the wolverine will drop the moss to the ground, and if the deer stops to eat it, the wolverine will drop onto the deer's head, bite it, and, says Allardyce, "tear its victim's eyes out."[12] Then in a fit of desperation, the deer blindly slams its head into the tree to get rid of the clinging wolverine, falls to the ground dead, and the wolverine eats it.

Researchers today say that such accounts are exaggerated and probably even untrue, but wolverines definitely have a bad reputation. Some Native American legends describe wolverines as smart and evil and an embodiment of the devil. French Canadians named the wolverine *carcajou*, which means "evil one." Other nicknames given to the wolverine include "nasty cat" and "woods devil." Even in modern times wolverines are described as amazingly savage and dangerous for their size. Allardyce writes of the wolverine, "He is a unique combination of viciousness, courage, and cunning. He is one of the most powerful, thievish, daring and efficient killing machines known to man."[13]

Researcher Mike Harrington rejects much of the wolverine lore. He says, "They've got such a bad rap. A lot of myths about them are way overblown . . . but they're just doing their thing, looking for food."[14] Even so, wolverines are impressive predators—truly tough, strong, and well equipped to satisfy their voracious appetites.

Chapter 5

Honey Badger

The honey badger is only slightly bigger than the average house cat, but it is so ferocious that it is listed in the *Guinness Book of World Records* as the "most fearless animal in the world."[15] Many wildlife experts call it the meanest animal in the world. The honey badger, also known as a ratel, has a reputation for being a nasty-tempered, vicious little predator that will attack and try to kill anything in its path and never give ground to any other animal. The South African army has even named a series of infantry armored fighting vehicles the Ratels. For a honey badger, it is kill or die trying every time.

Body Basics

The honey badger is a member of the same family as weasels, ferrets, otters, polecats, and martens and is similar in appearance to these relatives. It has a stocky, low-slung body with short legs and long front claws for digging, climbing trees, and defense. It has dense, coarse black fur on its underside and a wide band of white or silver down its back, making it look something like a skunk. Also like a skunk, it has anal glands that can release a powerful, smothering stench when the animal feels threatened. Honey badgers weigh between 15 and 29 pounds (7 to 13 kg) and are 23.5 to 30 inches

THE HONEY BADGER
AT A GLANCE

- **Scientific name:** *Mellivora capensis*
- **Scientific family:** Mustelidae
- **Range:** Africa, India, and the Middle East
- **Habitat:** Wide-ranging from semidesert to deciduous forests to grasslands
- **Average size:** Height 9.1 to 11 inches (23 to 28 cm) at shoulder
- **Diet:** Extremely varied, from insects to snakes to mammals
- **Life span:** Unknown in the wild; estimates of seven to eight years
- **Key features:** Uniquely loose and tough skin, covered with thick, coarse fur
- **Deadly because:** Fearless, fierce, tenacious, and tireless
- **Conservation status:** Least concern, but population decreasing

(60 to 77 cm) long. The thin, furred tail can be 8 to 12 inches (20 to 30 cm) in length.

Honey badgers have sharp teeth and powerful jaws that can crush bone or chomp through (and eat) a turtle shell. They have internal ears that look like little ridges buried under their skin and fur that can be unfolded when needed. But the honey badger's most remarkable feature is its uniquely thick, tough, and pliable skin. The skin is almost 0.25 inches (6 mm) thick. It is so tough that local people say that spears bounce off it, African porcupine quills cannot penetrate it, and even a machete does not completely slice through it. In addition, a honey badger's skin is extremely loose—so much so that the animal can twist around or rotate inside it and bite any predator that has dared to grab it. The honey badger is so perfectly built for defense that few predators will try to attack it, and it is so confident of its safety that it will confront and fight any animal that gets in its way. These same characteristics also make the honey badger a tough and fearless hunter.

Home and Habits

Honey badgers live throughout most of sub-Saharan Africa and in parts of the Middle East and Asia. They live mainly in semiarid, dry regions but are also found in grasslands and deciduous forests. They are generally

Honey badgers have a reputation for being nasty-tempered, vicious little predators. They will attack and kill any animal that gets in their way.

solitary predators, although females and young hunt together for about two years, and sometimes a male and female will hunt together during mating seasons. They have large territories. Males in the Kalahari area of Africa, for example, maintain ranges of more than 193 square miles (500 sq km), which overlap the territories of several females. Female territories are smaller, averaging about 39 square miles (100 sq km). They patrol their territories regularly, scent-marking periodically to warn other honey badgers away. They also have a deep, menacing growl that they use to warn off intruding honey badgers or other predators.

Because their territories are so large, honey badgers do not have home dens. Instead, they have several dens throughout their ranges that they either dig themselves or take over from other burrowing animals. Females move their cubs from den to den every two to five days. Both sexes can be active at any time of the day or night, depending on conditions such as cold or heat or disturbances. For instance, if humans are active in the area, honey badgers may hunt at night, while in wilderness areas far from people they may hunt by day.

On the Hunt

Honey badgers are generalist and opportunistic hunters, meaning that they will eat anything they happen across at any time. They will always eat when the opportunity arises, even when they have just had a big meal. As they travel, honey badgers use their excellent sense of smell to discover prey above or below ground in burrows, and any meal will do. Honey badgers hunt and eat small prey such as lizards, birds, insects, small rodents, and insect larvae. They will hunt larger prey such as crocodiles up to 3 feet (1 m) long, hares, polecats, juvenile foxes, young antelope, and snakes of any size. They will also eat carrion and steal carcasses from other predators.

As its name implies, the honey badger raids bee-hives, but it does not really want the honey. It tears

The honey badger uses its long, sharp claws for digging and climbing trees—and for defense. It can also release a powerful stench when threatened.

PROBLEM-SOLVING HONEY BADGERS

Honey badgers are not only fierce, they are intelligent. In the wild, they have been documented using tools. In one instance, a honey badger rolled a nearby log over to a site where a kingfisher was stuck in roots in an underground cave out of the badger's reach. The honey badger then stood on the log and grabbed the bird. Other badgers have rolled logs to fences to climb over the obstacles. They have been documented piling up several objects such as sticks and rocks to climb over walls. A honey badger named Stoffel lives at the South African Moholoholo Rehabilitation Centre and has caused havoc and destruction because his caretakers cannot build an enclosure that will hold him. He has escaped every cage, brick building, and fenced area, killing other animal residents and taking over the center's kitchens. He used shovels, rakes, stones, and his own dexterous claws to climb high walls, unlock gates, and open refrigerators. It seems that humans are no match for a honey badger's fearless determination.

hives apart to get at the bee larvae inside and gorge upon the larvae and the comb. Occasionally, a honey badger will be killed by multiple furious bee stings to its face, but most often it does not even seem to notice the hundreds of stings that would kill another animal or a human, leaving the hive only when it has been decimated. Since the eighteenth century, people have claimed that an African bird called the greater honeyguide leads the honey badger to beehives on purpose. The bird benefits because after the honey badger has eaten all it can, the greater honeyguide flies in and eats the leftover honey without having to break the hive open and without danger from the bees. Scientists doubt the truth of this association. No one has ever actually reported seeing a honeyguide lead a badger to a beehive. Instead, as Ed Yong of *National Geographic* points out, "It's possible that honeyguides follow the badgers to honey."[16] Honey badgers have no trouble finding hives by themselves.

Bee stings are not the only peril that honey badgers face with impunity when they are on the hunt. During summer months, more than 50 percent of a honey badger's diet is snakes, including large, deadly venomous snakes like puff adders, black mambas, and cobras. When it finds a snake, the honey badger immediately leaps on it and bites the snake's head and neck. Often the snake bites the badger, but amazingly it is not killed. It is protected by its tough skin, thick fur, and an innate resistance to the venom, surviving bites that would kill an elephant or dissolve human flesh. Resistance is not the same as immunity. Sometimes the snake's fangs do penetrate the honey badger's skin, especially on its face. At those times, the honey badger may fall into a coma-like state for minutes or hours, but somehow (scientists are not sure how) the badger throws off the effects of the venom, wakes up, and acts like nothing has happened. And if the honey badger managed to kill the snake (as usually happens) before it fell ill, it wakes to a delicious snake meal. It can devour a 5-foot (1.5 m) snake in minutes.

Honey badger experts Colleen and Keith Begg say,

> Snakes make high-yield meals, and honey bad-
> gers track them relentlessly. Wherever snakes try to
> hide—up trees, in dense brush, or underground—
> badgers follow and attack. . . . One night we saw a
> young male collapse. He'd been struck in the face
> by a puff adder just before he bit its head off. We
> expected that he would die. But after two hours he
> woke up, groggily finished his meal, and later trot-
> ted off into the sunrise.[17]

No Fear

The honey badger is a capable, courageous hunter, but
its toughness is just as obvious when it defends itself
or faces down other predators. Lions and leopards occasionally hunt honey badgers, but more often than not,
the badger wins the fight. When a lion grabs a honey
badger in its jaws, the badger can twist around inside its
skin and bite the lion on its face. There is almost no way
to grab a badger so that it cannot bite, and honey badgers are tireless. They can fight for their lives for hours,
often until the larger predator has to give up in exhaus-
tion. Many researchers say that only a young lion will try
to snatch a honey badger, and having once tried it, the
predator will avoid honey badgers in the future.

Honey badgers have been filmed standing up to lions
instead of running away when they had the chance. In
one film, two honey badgers walked right up to a pride of
six lions, almost as if daring them to object. The two old-
er lionesses (perhaps from experience) hung back, but

Two honey badgers face off against a pack of large canines known as African wild dogs. Honey badgers have been filmed standing up to—and attacking—lions.

the four younger lions attacked, and eventually the two lionesses joined in the fight. One lioness snatched one of the badgers in her jaws, clamping most of its body in her mouth. Twisting around, the badger viciously bit the lioness's nose so hard that she dropped the badger. The badger got up, turned around, and rushed at the lioness again. Giles Kelmanson, a South African game ranger, watched as the tenacious badgers kept attacking the pride. Even when the badgers could have escaped, they would return to attack the lions again. Kelmanson says, "They are such tough creatures and so ferocious that they managed to beat up the six lions. Incredible. Luckily both honey badgers got away, fairly unscathed. And I think the poor lioness was a little worse for wear."[18]

Fierce honey badger attacks on large herd animals such as water buffalo and zebras have also been reported. The honey badgers have been described as running underneath the big male animals and ripping off their testicles. Then the badgers wait for the animals to bleed to death and feast on them. Scientists cannot verify these stories, but they do add to the honey badger's reputation as a mean, bad-tempered animal that does not care who or what it has to fight as it hunts for its next meal.

Chapter 6

Spotted Hyena

Spotted hyenas have a reputation for being cowardly carrion eaters, but in reality they are bold and deadly predators—one of the top predators in Africa. They are also the most common predators on the African continent. While they are scavengers when the opportunity arises, these large, powerful pack animals actually hunt and kill up to 95 percent of the animals they eat. Spotted hyenas have also been known to attack and kill humans.

In 2003, in the mountainous Dowa region of Malawi, an unidentified animal terrorized villagers by killing and eating three people and mauling sixteen more. The three fatal attacks were on two elderly women and a three-year-old child, whose bodies were found with crushed skulls and devoured intestines and genitals. The surviving victims suffered missing legs, hands, ears, noses, and eyes. The "Malawi Terror Beast," as it came to be known, caused some four thousand villagers to flee their homes. Government officials were certain the animal was a rabid hyena and sent police and gamekeepers to the area to kill it. No one knows what happened to the mysterious animal. It disappeared and the attacks stopped, but many villagers insisted that the creature was not a real hyena. It looked like a big hyena, they claimed, but it was unnatural and monstrous. They insisted it was the evil spirit of a

THE SPOTTED HYENA AT A GLANCE

- **Scientific name:** *Crocuta crocuta*
- **Scientific family:** Hyaenidae
- **Range:** Much of sub-Saharan Africa
- **Habitat:** Diverse: Deserts, mountains, woodlands, and grasslands
- **Average size:** 2.3 to 3 feet (0.3 to 1 m) at shoulder.
- **Diet:** Mammal herbivores, birds, fish, reptiles, vegetable matter
- **Life span:** Up to twenty-five years
- **Key features:** Muscular neck, long forelegs, sloping back, bone-crushing teeth
- **Deadly because:** Skillful predator with stamina, powerful teeth, and the strength to disembowel prey
- **Conservation status:** Least concern

hyena that had been killed the year before and that it had returned from the dead to exact revenge upon them.

Whatever the truth about the Malawi Terror Beast, a rampaging hyena is a frightening and capable predator. Chris Wasserman, a South African nature writer, says of hyenas, "They are said to be the predators most likely to attack humans sleeping outside in the open."[19]

Body Basics

The spotted hyena is the largest of the three species of hyenas—and the most dangerous. Although hyenas look something like dogs and something like cats, they are related to neither and are in a family of their own. They have sandy- to grayish-brown, coarse, woolly fur that is covered with black or brown spots; rounded ears; and a thin tail with a bushy tip. Hyenas weigh between 99 and 187 pounds (45 to 85 kg). The females are bigger than the males. Spotted hyenas have longer forelegs than hind legs and long, muscular necks so that their backs slope downward toward the tail. This structure gives the hyenas the strength to carry (rather than have to drag) large portions of meat when necessary. They have unusually large, strong hearts for their size,

The spotted hyena (pictured) is the largest and most powerful of all the hyenas. Hyenas will run through a group of grazing animals, pick one, and then chase it for long distances before making the kill.

which enables them to run for miles at a time without tiring. Hyenas also have powerful jaws with carnassial teeth for slicing meat and crushing bone. Hyenas eat so much bone that their feces are a chalky white.

Spotted hyenas have been condemned in many societies for centuries as devilish or demonic, in part because of their frequent, raucous vocalizations. They are also called "laughing hyenas" because of the weird, cackling, wailing noises they make when communicating with each other and a kind of giggle they emit when they are nervous. The eerie sounds seem otherworldly to humans.

Home and Habits

Spotted hyenas are abundantly distributed throughout most of sub-Saharan Africa. They live in grasslands, swamplands, semideserts, forests, and mountainous regions. They are highly social animals, living in groups called clans, ranging in size from as few as three to as many as ninety individuals. Females are dominant and maintain a hierarchy, with each female holding a rank, from the leader down to the lowest-ranking individual. The lowest-ranking female can be pushed around and dominated by all the other females. Females do not necessarily fight for dominance; instead, they inherit their ranks from their mothers. All the females are dominant over all the males, but each male has his own rank among the males.

Females usually remain in the clan for life, although not all the females in a clan are related. About four or five unrelated females usually form a clan together. Males tend to leave the clan when they are around two years old and join other clans, where they may be preferred

SIBLICIDE

Siblicide is the killing of one member of a litter by another. Spotted hyenas have just one or two cubs at a time, and on occasion the stronger cub kills the other. When spotted hyena cubs are born, their eyes are open and they have a full set of teeth. Almost from birth, the cubs begin to fight for dominance. Often the weaker cub ends up injured or scarred from this aggression, and it sometimes dies.

Scientists have different theories about the benefits of early fighting in hyena cubs. Some say that siblicide occurs when the mother is starving and cannot produce enough milk for two cubs. Other scientists say that it can happen because one of the mother's nipples has been damaged in a fight so that she can nurse only one cub. Still other scientists point out that single cubs have been observed to grow faster and bigger than twin cubs, so perhaps becoming a singleton helps the survivor reach adulthood. Siblicide may be nature's way of ensuring that only the strongest cubs live to join the clan and mate in adulthood. Whatever the answer, it seems that spotted hyenas have evolved to practice violence from birth.

as mates over the resident clan members. The clans are tight-knit but quarrelsome. Clan members push, shove, threaten, and fight with each other frequently, but they remain loyal to the clan; most form alliances and coalitions with other clan members that seem like friendships.

All the members of a clan do not stay together all the time. They often go off alone or in small groups for days at a time and then return to the clan after hunting or exploratory trips. The entire clan, however, defends its territory together, defends the clan den, and cooperates to protect kills from other predators.

On the Hunt

Spotted hyenas may hunt alone, in a small group, or as an entire clan. Their preferred prey includes antelope of all sizes, zebra, wildebeest, buffalo, warthog, and the young of giraffe, hippopotamus, and rhinoceros. A group of hyenas usually hunts by running through a group of grazing animals and choosing an individual to attack. They then chase the prey animal for long distances, with one or more hyenas nipping at the hind legs until finally the animal turns to face its predator. At that point the other hyenas go for the prey's belly and bite out chunks. Shortly after this, the encircled animal is disemboweled. Hyenas may also hunt resting wildebeest or deer with surprise attacks.

Spotted hyenas are opportunistic feeders that often eat carrion or steal kills from other predators. They find these meals by scent from up to 2.5 miles (4 km) away, by sight, such as watching for vultures, and hearing, such as the noises made during a kill. If another predator is able to drive a hyena from its kill, it can first tear away and run off with a large hunk of the carcass. Lions often steal hyena kills. Hyenas can steal carcasses from lions, but only if they outnumber the lions by at least four to one. Spotted hyenas will make a meal of almost anything. They have been observed eating flamingos and devouring buffalo dung. When their territories overlap with humans, they will raid garbage dumps and eat domestic animals such as donkeys, goats, and sheep. In the Masai tribe of Kenya and Tanzania, the traditional

The jaws and teeth of the spotted hyena are made for slicing meat and crushing bone. Once hyenas trap an animal, they bite chunks of flesh from its belly and then disembowel it.

practice when someone has died is not to bury the body but to rub it with animal fat and blood and then carry it to the bush for predators to eat. When hyenas find these corpses, they eat human flesh, too.

When Hyenas Attack Humans

Spotted hyena attacks on humans are rare but probably underreported. Every year a few people in Africa are mauled or killed by a hyena. In 2012, for example, a family sleeping in a hut in rural Kenya was attacked by a pack of hyenas. Two children were killed and six other people were mauled. The Kenyan Wildlife Service sent rangers to kill the hyenas, but it says that such attacks are becoming more common as the human population increases and encroaches upon hyena territory.

In another tragic case in 2014, two children in Tanzania were attacked and killed by a lone hyena while they were playing outside in their small village. In that

A spotted hyena (photographed in a national park in Kenya, Africa) walks with its kill—a flamingo. Hyenas will eat almost anything, including carcasses they steal from other animals.

same year, a man was walking alone at night through a wildlife sanctuary in northern Yemen when he was attacked and killed by a hyena. He was on the phone with his wife at the time and she heard him scream for help. She alerted their sons who rushed to the scene, but explained a police spokesman, "When the sons reached him, it was too late. They only found the head and feet of their father."[20]

As they do with their normal prey, spotted hyenas go for weak, vulnerable, and isolated humans. The scientists and conservationists of the Hyaena Specialist Group explain,

> Each year a very small number of Africans are mauled or killed by spotted hyenas in rural areas, most frequently when sleeping unprotected in the bush or moving about in the bush near dawn or dusk. Occasionally a hyaena will contract rabies and attack in broad daylight. Occasionally spotted hyaenas have been known to enter tents and drag out a human from the interior, but only under two special circumstances: when the tent is left unzipped or when meat is also present inside the tent with the attacked person.[21]

Experts believe that most attacks are the result of the pressures of increased human presence in wild areas, loss of habitat, and a scarcity of natural prey.

In some cases, spotted hyenas and humans can cautiously coexist with each other. In Addis Ababa, Ethiopia, about a thousand urban hyenas live in and around the city, scavenge the dumps, eat feral cat and stray dog populations, and at times raid shallow graves in public cemeteries. Sometimes they attack homeless people sleeping in the streets at night. Periodically authorities cull the hyena packs, destroying their dens and killing the animals living too close to thickly populated human areas, but there is no exterminating the hyenas altogether. James Jeffrey, a resident of the city, says, "Their bite is stronger than that of a great white shark, and they're reviled and feared in many countries, but in Ethiopia there is a long tradition of people and hyenas living side-by-side, tolerating each other."[22] Humans and hyenas may learn to tolerate each other, but people never know when the dynamic might change. Wherever they live, spotted hyenas are dangerous enough that an attack is an ever-present possibility.

Source Notes

Chapter 1: Lion

1. Craig Packer, "Rational Fear," *Natural History Magazine*. www.naturalhistorymag.com.
2. Quoted in Christine Dell'Amore, "Tour Guide Killed in Lion Attack Did Everything Right," *National Geographic*, August 26, 2015. http://news.nationalgeographic.com.

Chapter 2: Tiger

3. Jim Corbett, *Man Eaters of Kumaon*. London: Oxford University Press, 1944, p. xii. https://archive.org.
4. Corbett, *Man Eaters of Kumaon*, p. x.
5. Quoted In Jeffrey Hays, "Tigers That Attack Humans," Facts and Details, 2008. http://factsanddetails.com.
6. Quoted in Monotosh Chakraborty, "Tiger Snatches Man Off Boat, Leaps Back into Sunderbans Jungle," *The Times of India*, June 27, 2014. http://timesofindia.indiatimes.com.

Chapter 3: Polar Bear

7. Quoted in Jonathan Amos, "Polar Bear 'Cannibalism' Pictured," BBC News, December 12, 2011. www.bbc.com.
8. Quoted in Jake Abrahamson, "The Man Who Survived a Polar Bear Attack," Sierra, January/February 2015. www.sierraclub.org.

Chapter 4: Wolverine

9. Quoted in Riley Woodford, "Study of Tough, Cunning Alaska Wolverine Dispels Some Myths," Alaska Dispatch News, January 25, 2015. www.adn.com.

10. Wildlife Conservation Society. "When Predators Attack (Each Other): Researchers Document First-Known Killing of a Wolverine by a Black Bear in Yellowstone." ScienceDaily, May 6, 2003. www.sciencedaily.com.

11. Quoted in Alex Heigl, "Man Survives 3 Days Lost in Alaskan Wilderness, Fends Off Wolverine," *People*, December 28, 2014. www.people.com.

12. Quoted in Mark Allardyce, *Wolverine: A Look into the Devil's Eyes* (eBook), Rainy Day Projects, 2005, p. 21. https://books.google.com.

13. Allardyce, *Wolverine*, p. 20.

14. Quoted in Woodford, "Study of Tough, Cunning Alaska Wolverine."

Chapter 5: Honey Badger

15. Quoted in The Honey Badger. www.honeybadger.com.

16. Ed Yong, "Lies, Damned Lies, and Honey Badgers," *National Geographic*, September 19, 2011. http://phenomena.nationalgeographic.com.

17. Colleen and Keith Begg, "Honey Badgers," *National Geographic*, September 2004. http://ngm.nationalgeographic.com.

18. Giles Kelmanson, *Badger Bravery* (video), Nat Geo Wild. http://channel.nationalgeographic.com.

Chapter 6: Spotted Hyena

19. Chris Wasserman, "Hyena Facts: Is This a Cowardly Scavenger or an Efficient Hunter?," Africa Wildlife Detective, 2010–2016. www.africa-wildlife-detective .com.
20. Quoted in "Yemeni Told Wife on Phone He Was Being Devoured by Hyena," Emirates 24/7 News, March 23, 2014. www.emirates247.com.
21. "Frequently Asked Questions About Hyaenas," Hyaena Specialist Group, 2007–2016. www.hyaenidae .org.
22. James Jeffrey, "Running with the Hyenas of Addis Ababa," Wardheer News, March 5, 2016. www.ward heernews.com.

Glossary

anal glands: Small, paired sac-like glands on either side of the anus in many mammals that contain an oily fluid that can be discharged.

blubber: The fat layer of sea mammals.

boreal: Of northern, cold regions with short summers and snowy winters.

carnassial: The large molar and premolar teeth of a carnivore adapted for shearing and cutting flesh.

carrion: Decaying animal flesh.

circumpolar: Located around one of the earth's poles.

compensatory predation: Preying on those animals that would have died of some other cause and thus not affecting the overall population of prey animals.

hierarchy: Social organization in which individuals are ranked one above the other according to status, strength, or importance.

indigenous: Native to or occurring naturally in a certain location.

intraspecific: Within a species.

omnivorous: Eating both plant and animal foods.

opportunistic: Taking advantage of opportunities as they occur and of whatever circumstances are available.

rabid: Infected with rabies, a serious, fatal disease of the nervous system.

scavenger: An animal that feeds on dead and decaying animals and/or vegetable matter.

subspecies: Populations of animals living in particular geographic regions and having distinguishable characteristics that separate them from other populations of the species, even though all are capable of interbreeding.

Books

Alain Bergeron, *Do You Know Hyenas?* Markham, Ontario, Canada: Fitzhenry & Whiteside, 2014.

Robert Coupe, *Cats of the Wild.* Silver Spring, MD: Discovery Education, 2015.

Kitson Jazynka, *Mission: Tiger Rescue: All About Tigers and How to Save Them.* Des Moines, IA: National Geographic Children's Books, 2015.

Joe McDonald, *World's Deadliest Creatures.* London: Reed New Holland Publishers, 2016.

Glenn Murphy, *Predators: The Whole Tooth-and-Claw Story.* London: Macmillan Children's Books, 2015.

Rebecca Stefoff, *Polar Bears.* New York: Cavendish Square Publishing, 2014.

Websites

ALERT (http://lionalert.org). This website is dedicated to providing information about African lions and working for lion conservation.

The Honey Badger (www.honeybadger.com). Explore this website dedicated to honey badgers and learn about their lives and remarkable behaviors.

Hyaena Specialist Group (www.hyaenidae.org). Learn about all the species of hyenas, extinct and living. Click the "Just for Kids" link to discover interesting hyena facts (and why Europeans spell the word with an extra *a*).

Polar Boars International (www.polarbearsinternation al.org). This is the only conservation organization dedicated exclusively to polar bears and their survival. The site has a link for students and much information about polar bears and their habitat.

Tigers-World (www.tigers-world.com). Visitors to this site can learn about tiger conservation, tiger behavior, tiger interactions with humans, and the types of tigers still living in the world.

The Wolverine Foundation (www.wolverinefoundation .org). Dedicated to preserving and conserving wolverines, the foundation provides detailed descriptions of wolverines and their lives. Click the "Resources" link to learn all about this remarkable animal.

Video

Honey Badgers: Stealing Dinner from a Snake (http:// channel.nationalgeographic.com/videos/dangerous-dining). National Geographic Channel video wherein a honey badger steals a rodent out of a venomous snake's mouth, eats the rodent, decides to attack the snake, and is bitten. Watch what happens next with film and commentary by Keith and Colleen Begg.

Index

Picture Credits

Cover: Shutterstock.com/Michal Ninger

7: © Sergey Gorshkov/Minden Pictures

11: Depositphotos

14: © Andrew Harrington/NPL/Minden Photos

16: © Mitsuaki Iwago/Minden Pictures

19: © Konrad Wothe/Minden Pictures

22: © Pete Oxford/NPL/Minden Pictures

24: © Patricio Robles Gil/Minden Pictures

28: © Matthias Breiter/Minden Pictures

31: © Flip Nicklin/Minden Pictures

35: © Rhinie van Meurs/NIS/Minden Pictures

39: © Sergey Gorshkov/NPL/Minden Pictures

41: Design Pics/Robert Postma/Newscom

44: © Igor Shpilenok/NPL/Minden Pictures

49: Depositphotos

51: © Ann and Steve Toon/NPL/Minden Pictures

55: © Suzi Eszterhas/Minden Pictures

59: Tony Camacho/Science Source

63: © Suzi Eszterhas/Minden Pictures

64: Winifried Wisniewski/Minden Pictures/Newscom

About The Author

Toney Allman holds degrees from Ohio State University and the University of Hawaii. She currently lives in Virginia, where she enjoys a rural lifestyle as well as researching and writing about a variety of topics for students.